Set 1   Clothes to Wear   (Voc

sneakers	jeans	petticoat	
bootees	trunks	rompers	pyjamas
slippers	gloves	sweater	uniform
thongs	veil	bikini	sandal

(1)   Baby wears a pair of woollen .... on his or her feet.

(2)   A boy goes for a swim in a pair of ....

(3)   A bride sometimes wears a .... over her face.

(4)   Boys and girls wear strong pants that are called ....

(5)   In winter you wear a pullover which is also a ....

(6)   Boys and sometimes girls go to bed in a pair of ....

(7)   A person in the police or armed forces wears a special ....

(8)   A child about two years old plays in a pair of ....

(9)   A very small girl's bathing suit is a ....

(10) People wear rubber .... on their feet in summer.

(11) Mother wears a .... under her dress.

(12) .... are soft shoes worn in the home.

(13) Rubber-soled shoes for playing sport are called ....

(14) A type of open leather shoe is a ....

(15) We can put .... on our hands to keep warm.

Owls are birds with large eyes. They see well in the dark. Their feathers are soft and fluffy. The fluffed up feathers make them seem larger than they are. Have you heard a hooting noise at night? This was probably an owl. The father and mother owl are not good nest builders. They usually find a hole in an old dead tree. Up to seven white eggs are laid. The mother sits on the eggs until they hatch. The father then has to spend much time hunting for food to feed the new babies. He will try to catch mice, frogs or insects. He likes to look for food during the night when it is dark. He flies from tree to tree and sits very still in the branches, listening for sounds. Perhaps a mouse will be eating some seeds in the grass. Then, having spotted his prey, he flies down quietly. With his sharp claws he picks up the dinner.

(1)   Owls see well in the ....

    ....

(2)   Fluffy feathers make them seem ....

    ....

(3)   Owls make a .... noise.

    ....

(4)   Owls like to nest in an old .... tree.

    ....

(5)   An owl uses its .... to carry food.

    ....

(6)   **The mother owl lays up to .... eggs.**

    ....

(7)   Write the names of the three creatures that owls eat.

    ....

Set 3   Crossword   (Spelling and Vocabulary)

Across
1 We live in one.
3 used for sweeping
5 Campers sleep in it.
7 Ships sail on it.
9 three plus three
10 a boat that pulls other boats
12 It goes on your head
14 People ride in one.
15 not late
16 It makes honey.
18 not sad
20 We use them to run.
22 A ..... grows to be a woman.

Down
1 not cold
2 You ..... in a chair.
4 Cats chase them.
6 a bird's home
8 You can chop wood with it.
11 not down
13 We bite with them.
14 A dog loves a ..... .
16 It can bounce.
17 A hen lays it.
19 an animal that grunts
21 Ice is ..... cold.

Set 4   Food and Drink   (Vocabulary)

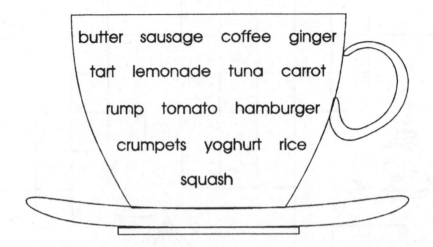

butter   sausage   coffee   ginger

tart   lemonade   tuna   carrot

rump   tomato   hamburger

crumpets   yoghurt   rice

squash

(1)   A .... is a pastry filled with fruit or jam.

(2)   .... is a drink made of roasted and crushed beans.

(3)   .... is made from cream and we spread it on bread.

(4)   Minced meat that is fried and put in a bun is a ....

(5)   .... is a grain that can be eaten with curry.

(6)   .... is a canned fish we buy in the supermarket.

(7)   A .... is a red salad fruit also made into sauce.

(8)   .... is a hot spice made from a plant root.

(9)   .... is a drink made of crushed oranges or lemons.

(10) A .... is a vegetable that grows under the ground.

(11) .... is a dairy food made from sour milk.

(12) We toast and put butter on ....

(13) .... is a cut of beef from the back of a beast.

(14) Chopped meat and other foods put into a skin makes a ....

(15) .... is a fizzy drink sold in cans or bottles.

Set 5   Pirates   (Spelling in Context)

Today if you travel by ship no pirates will rob you. Long ago it was not so safe. Pirates with guns, swords and daggers sailed the seas. They made a living by robbing ships and stealing any money or cargo aboard. The poor people on these ships were often killed or held to ransom. The pirate's flag was the 'Jolly Roger'. It was black, with a white skull on it. Under the skull were two crossed bones. Pirates stored their stolen gold, silver or jewels in chests. When a pirate ship came to a lonely island, these men often buried their chests full of treasure. A map was drawn to show the exact spot where the treasure was hidden under the ground. In England, pirates were hunted by ships of the Royal Navy. If a pirate was captured he was hanged at a special place in the port of London.

(1)   Long ago there were .... who robbed ships.

(2)   Many .... on these ships were killed.

(3)   The 'Jolly Roger' had crossed bones under a white ....

(4)   Pirates chose .... islands to bury their chests.

(5)   A map was drawn to show where the chests were ....

(6)   Besides using swords and guns, pirates could kill with ....

(7)   The colour of a pirate flag was ....

(8)   Ships of the Royal .... hunted pirates.

(9)   Pirates who were caught were .... in London.

(10) Write the three valuable things that pirates stole.

      ....

Set 6   Crossword   (Spelling and Vocabulary)

Across

1   a baby dog
3   You can put money in it.
6   a large fierce cat-like animal
7   It can ring.
8   It is wet.
11   not even
12   They are built around houses.
14   Ducks swim on it.
16   opposite to 'stop'
20   not cheap
21   used in the garden

Down

2   a colour
4   Be ..... to animals.
5   He or she works in a school.
7   It has wings.
9   Water comes from it.
10   A cat will chase one.
12   It makes a croaking sound.
13   worn on the head
15   You open it.
17   Grandmothers are ..... .
18   A horse can ..... .
19   You sleep on it.
22   We eat bread ..... butter.

Set 7   Doing Words (Verbs)   (Vocabulary)

> haul raise forget stroll slide repair construct shove
> cry stack worry choose approach relax tumble tiptoe
> prepare decide bustle reason

(1) We .... when we are in pain.

(2) We .... when we are in no hurry and walk slowly.

(3) We .... things on top of each other.

(4) We .... when we rest or stop working.

(5) We .... when we skate on ice.

(6) We .... things when we mend them.

(7) We .... when we fall.

(8) We .... when we feel uneasy about something.

(9) We .... things when we build them.

(10) We .... when we try to work out a problem.

(11) We .... when we walk and try not to make a sound.

(12) We .... things when we lift them.

(13) We .... things when we make them ready.

(14) We .... when we come nearer.

(15) We .... when we make up our minds.

(16) We .... when we are in a hurry.

(17) We .... when we pull things.

(18) We .... when we push people or things.

(19) We .... when we pick or select from two or more things.

(20) We .... when we do not remember.

Set 8   Giraffes   (Spelling in Context)

Giraffes are the tallest animals in the world. They live in Africa. A large giraffe grows to be five metres high. Even a baby giraffe is nearly two metres when it is born. A giraffe eats leaves and twigs from trees. It chews its cud like the cow. This animal has a light brown patchy coat which makes it hard to see in the shadow of trees. Two small tufted horns grow between its ears. To drink, a giraffe parts its front legs and then bends its long neck downwards. Giraffes see very well. They keep a close watch for lions that try to kill them. Luckily, giraffes have very long legs so they can move quickly. Their legs are also useful for kicking. Lions and other attackers, like cheetahs, have been killed by strong kicks from giraffes.

Have you ever seen a giraffe walking? Next time you go to the zoo, watch carefully. Both legs move on one side and then both legs move on the other.

(1)   Giraffes live in the continent of ....

(2)   A baby giraffe is two .... tall.

(3)   The coat of a giraffe is light brown and ....

(4)   A giraffe's horns are short and ....

(5)   Giraffes are attacked by .... and cheetahs.

     Write each word that means:

(6)   fortunately ....

(7)   almost ....

(8)   lookout ....

(9)   difficult ....

Set 9 Crossword (Spelling and Vocabulary)

Across
1 It makes us wet.
3 seven days
4 A can may be made of ..... .
5 Flowers grow in it.
10 We walk in them.
11 a baby cow
13 You eat it with jam.
15 not out
17 A cowboy has one.
20 Cows eat it.
21 You can write with one.

Down
1 It goes on a finger.
2 A dog or cat is a ..... .
4 not short
6 stone
7 You smell with it .
8 Bob cut ..... own foot.
9 used to clean up with water
11 You drink from it.
12 It swims well.
14 A girl wears one.
16 used on a clothes line
18 not shut
19 used to hold chips

Set 10   Books and Stories   (Vocabulary)

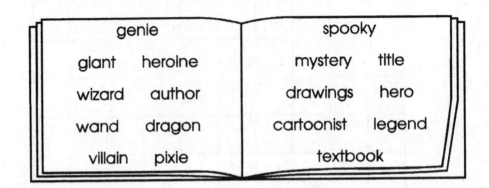

genie

glant   herolne

wizard   author

wand   dragon

villain   pixie

spooky

mystery   title

drawings   hero

cartoonist   legend

textbook

(1)   The name of a book on the cover is the ....

(2)   The person who writes a book is the ....

(3)   Pictures drawn inside books are illustrations or ....

(4)   The most important boy or man in the story is the ....

(5)   A .... is a person who has magic powers.

(6)   A wicked person in a story is the ....

(7)   Another name for a fairy or an elf is a ....

(8)   A .... is a story about something secret or unknown.

(9)   A creature in old stories that breathed fire was a ....

(10)   When Aladdin rubbed his lamp a spirit or .... appeared.

(11)   A large person in a fairy story is a ....

(12)   A book used in the classroom at school is a ....

(13)   A person who draws funny pictures in books is a ....

(14)   A fairy waves a .... to cast a spell.

(15)   A very old story handed down is a fable or ....

(16)   A story about ghosts could be ....

(17)   The most important girl or woman in a story is the ....

Set 11   Leopards   (Spelling in Context)

Leopards are cats. They are large and wild. Only lions and tigers are larger cats. The usual coat of a leopard is a light tan colour with many black spots that are close together. A leopard climbs a tree and sits waiting to spring. When an animal walks past, it will jump down to kill it. The spots on a leopard's coat make the animal hard to see. They blend in with leaves of trees which also look like spots with the sun shining through.

Leopards like to eat monkeys or deer. They usually leave people alone, but once a leopard has attacked a human then this animal becomes very dangerous. It is so cunning that it will wait for hours and stalk a person who may be unaware of the danger and be taken by surprise. Today there are few leopards. Many have been hunted for their skins. The fur made warm coats for women. Today we are trying to stop coats being made from leopard skins.

(1)   Leopards are wild ....

(2)   Leopards sit in ....

(3)   It is hard to see a leopard as its .... look like ....

(4)   A leopard is smaller than a lion or a ....

(5)   Leopards were hunted for their ....

(6)   Leopard fur made .... for women.

(7)   Today we are .... to stop using leopard skins.

(8)   Animals that leopards eat include deer and ....

     Write each word that means:

(9)   big ....   (10) leap ....

(11) **crafty or shrewd** ....   (12) difficult ....

Set 12   Crossword   (Spelling and Vocabulary)

Across

1   a small insect
5   It grows and smells nice.
7   It likes to gallop.
8   a very large animal
12   I can be open or shut.
13   opposite to 'day'
14   Mother is a ..... .
16   water that flows
18   Girls play with them.
20   He used to bring everyone milk.
23   to hit with the hand
24   a baby goat
25   You hear with them.

Down

1   a fruit you eat
2   The sun gives you a ..... .
3   many times
4   I bark.
6   My ears are long.
9   I was once a tree.
10   I ..... my dog.
11   five plus five
14   You look out of them.
15   Houses can be made of them.
17   Cars stop at a ..... light.
19   made when fires burn
21   A hammer hits it on the head.
22   used to fry eggs and bacon

Set 13   Homes and Buildings   (Vocabulary)

garage sampan igloo cottage wigwam hospital
cinema palace mansion factory caravan church
chalet motel   unit duplex
penthouse   terrace-house

(1) An Eskimo's home is called an ....

(2) A home in the same building as others is a flat or ....

(3) A Red Indian's home is a tepee or ....

(4) A small house, especially in the country, is called a ....

(5) A house that is large and expensive is a ....

(6) A Chinese boat that is used as a home is a ....

(7) A house that is attached to others each side is a ....

(8) A car is kept in a car-port or ....

(9) A building where people worship God is a ....

(10) Sick people are treated in a ....

(11) The home of a King and Queen is a ....

(12) A place to stop the night on a journey is a ....

(13) A large flat on the top of a building is a ....

(14) A building where things are made is a ....

(15) A building in which you can watch films is a ....

(16) A small house built near snow for skiers is a ....

(17) A home that is on wheels and can be towed is a ....

(18) Two separate houses built on top of each other is a ....

Set 14 Once Bitten Twice Shy (Spelling from Context)

There are lots of sayings that we use. 'Once bitten, twice shy' is just one saying. It means that if we have been tricked or caught once, we will not be tricked again. This is an old Greek story.

A dog was once lying in the sun. He was near a gate on his master's farm. A wolf crept up and jumped on the dog. The wolf fastened his teeth on the dog's neck. 'Look how thin I am,' wailed the dog. 'My master is going to feed me soon. Wait until I become fatter. Then you may eat me.'

The wolf thought this was a good idea. He went away. Soon the wolf returned. He spotted the dog asleep on the roof of the farm house.

'Come down,' shouted the wolf, so I can eat you.'
'No,' replied the dog. 'If you find me near the gate again, you may eat me. Once bitten twice shy!'

(1) 'Once bitten, twice shy' is a ....

(2) The dog was .... in the sun.

(3) The wolf was going to .... the dog.

(4) The dog told the wolf that he was ....

(5) When the wolf returned the dog was on the ....

(6) It was the .... who said, 'once bitten, twice shy'.

(7) The dog told the wolf he could eat him if he was near the

     .... again.

     Write the words that mean:

(8) walked up quietly ....   (9) spied ....

(10) made a fool of ....   (11) came back ....

Set 15   Crossword   (Spelling and Vocabulary)

Across
1 Your mother's mother.
5 It tastes nice.
7 A ..... light is not bright.
8 You ..... with your eyes.
9 A peanut is one.
11 He stops drivers that speed.
12 Every morning you eat ..... .
16 oppposite to 'no'
19 Cars run on it.
20 ..... things make us laugh
21 a fast plane

Down
1 opposite to 'bad'
2 A horse is an ..... .
3 It goes 'quack quack'.
4 It makes a car go.
6 opposite to 'odd'
8 Shops ..... things.
10 many houses make up a ..... .
12 a very young person
13 It flies from a pole.
14 a large fierce jungle cat
15 a yellow metal
17 opposite to 'hard'
18 You see with them.

Set 16　　　At School　(Vocabulary)

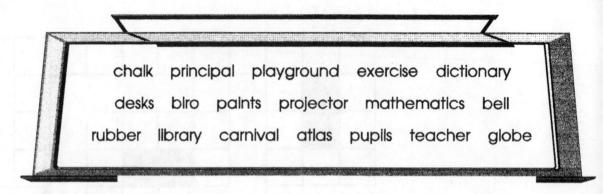

chalk　principal　playground　exercise　dictionary
desks　biro　paints　projector　mathematics　bell
rubber　library　carnival　atlas　pupils　teacher　globe

(1)　The school .... rings when it is time for school to begin.

(2)　We often write in an .... book.

(3)　The teacher writes with .... on the blackboard.

(4)　The person in charge of a school is the ....

(5)　To check the spelling of a word we use a ....

(6)　We use a .... to write words and sentences.

(7)　During some art lessons we use .... with brushes.

(8)　We see pictures on a screen with an overhead ....

(9)　When we add and subtract numbers we are doing ....

(10)　In a classroom children sit at tables or ....

(11)　Children at school are called ....

(12)　To alter writing or pencil drawing we use a ....

(13)　There are books for us to read and borrow in the ....

(14)　The best runners at school will race at the district ....

(15)　During play or recess we go into the ....

(16)　A book full of maps is called an ....

(17)　A round map of the world is called a ....

(18)　A person in charge of a class is a ....

Set 17   Space   (Spelling in Context)

When you look up into the sky you are looking into space. It lies between stars and planets. We think that space never ends. It stretches on and on past stars and planets that can only be seen by large telescopes.In space it is black. The only light comes from stars like the Sun which are burning.

Some men and women travel in space.They ride in a space-ship which is carried by a rocket that blasts off from Earth with a roar of flame and smoke. Their space-ship goes into orbit. They go round and round the Earth where there is no pull of gravity. Inside the ship the people float around. Food and water floats too and cannot be left on a table. To drink, a person squeezes water into the mouth.

One day men and women will travel far into space to reach other planets like Mars and Venus.

(1)   Space lies between stars and ....

(2)   Large .... are used to see distant stars.

(3)   Space is .... in colour.

(4)   Travellers in space ride in a ....

(5)   A .... blasts off from Earth.

(6)   The pull towards Earth is called ....

(7)   Objects inside a space-craft .... around if they are left loose.

(8)   Two planets mentioned are Mars and ....

     Write each word that means:

(9)   stops ....   (10) on fire ....

(11) the opposite of 'outside' ....

(12) the opposite of 'can' ....

Set 18   Crossword   (Spelling and Vocabulary)

Across
2 opposite of 'inside'
5 It sails on the sea.
6 You ..... with a knife.
7 We ..... with our ears.
9 You can eat roast ..... for dinner.
11 the Father of Jesus
12 You can ..... with a rope.
13 part of a bird's wing
15 opposite of 'happy'
16 a word that joins words
18 Seals ..... on fish.
20 not old
21 You can ..... flowers.
23 They fly in the sky.

Down
1 short word meaning 'taxi'
2 a round fruit
3 A snail lives in one.
4 A fire ..... .
8 ill
9 You can drink from one.
10 ..... 3 and 3 to make 6
13 It burns.
14 Bees make it.
15 five plus two
17 all the time
19 It is ..... at night.
22 not out

Set 19   Farming (Vocabulary)

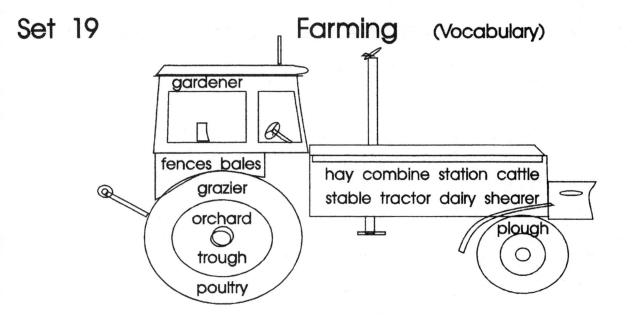

gardener

fences bales

grazier

orchard

trough

poultry

hay combine station cattle
stable tractor dairy shearer

plough

(1) A large farm in Australia is called a ....

(2) We get beef from ....

(3) A .... clips the wool from the sheep.

(4) Milk is produced on a .... farm.

(5) Hens, turkeys and geese are called ....

(6) Fruit trees growing together form an ....

(7) Before growing crops a farmer must .... the ground.

(8) Farmers use a .... to harvest wheat.

(9) A farmer that runs cattle or sheep is called a ....

(10) A person who grows vegetables is a market ....

(11) Horses shelter inside a ....

(12) A pig on a farm feeds from a ....

(13) A .... is used to pull a plough.

(14) Cattle are prevented from straying by ....

(15) Wool is pressed into .... before being sold.

(16) Grass cut in summer for winter feed is called ....

Set 20   The Eskimo   (Spelling in Context)

One day it was very cold. Small flakes of snow were beginning to fall. Susan was out in the garden. She came to the back door and said: 'I'm as cold as an Eskimo.' No wonder Susan used these words because an Eskimo lives where it is very cold. There is usually ice on the ground but Eskimo people try not to become cold. They wear warm clothes- often made from furs. Boys and girls have long pants that fit snugly into fur or woollen boots. Their fur coats have hoods. No cold air can come in and no warm air can go out.

It is even warm inside a snowhouse or igloo. The walls are made from blocks of ice but cold air cannot enter as there are no windows. The door is at the end of a narrow tunnel. Lamps and heaters which burn oil make it snug and cosy. Susan should have said: 'I wish I was as warm as an Eskimo!'

(1)   Flakes of .... were falling in Susan's garden.

(2)   Ice covers the .... where an Eskimo walks.

(3)   Eskimo clothes are mostly made of ....

(4)   An Eskimo wears a pair of .... on his or her feet.

(5)   A hood helps keep the .... air out.

(6)   An igloo is made from .... of ice.

(7)   Inside an igloo are lamps and heaters which burn ....

     Write the words that mean:

(8)   normally ....   (9)   come in ....

(10) the opposite of 'front' ....

(11) the opposite of 'cool' ....

(12) the opposite of 'seldom' ....

Set 21   Crossword   (Spelling and Vocabulary)

Across
2 People go there on Sundays.
4 happy
6 You can ..... your hands together.
7 A car has four of these.
10 a father sheep
11 We ..... on ice.
12 my father's father
17 ..... were all babies once.
18 Thunder makes a loud ..... .
21 nearly
23 Baby likes to ..... in the bath.

Down
1 You pour milk from one.
2 A large town is called a ..... .
3 not sad
5 You wash them after a meal.
8 Yesterday we ..... a fire.
9 a cat's foot
12 Grass is ..... .
13 a limb
14 opposite to 'thin'
15 A car beeps its ..... .
16 Horses run in ..... .
19 frozen water
20 A Penguin ..... fish.
22 Ice cubes ..... .

Set 22   Land Transport   (Vocabulary)

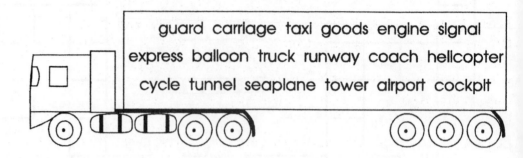

guard carriage taxi goods engine signal express balloon truck runway coach helicopter cycle tunnel seaplane tower airport cockpit

(1)   A .... train does not carry passengers.

(2)   A .... is a car that you hire to take you somewhere.

(3)   An aircraft that can land without a runway is a ....

(4)   An air .... is filled with gas and carries people.

(5)   A motor .... has two wheels and can go fast.

(6)   The .... rides in a special van at the back of a train.

(7)   Planes land and take off on the airport ....

(8)   A .... is able to take off and land on water.

(9)   To make a flight you catch a plane at the ....

(10)   A .... carries goods by road across the country.

(11)   A fast train is called an ....

(12)   People in the control .... allow planes to come and go.

(13)   A train runs through a .... instead of climbing a hill.

(14)   The .... of a train pulls the carriages.

(15)   A .... by the track tells the driver if the way is clear.

(16)   The .... of a train has seats for people.

(17)   A motor .... takes people to places by road.

(18)   The pilot of a plane sits in the ....

Set 23   Balloons For Flying   (Spelling in Context)

The first men to make a balloon were French. They filled a bag with hot air and from it they hung a basket. The first passengers to go for a ride in the air were animals. A duck, a rooster and a sheep sailed through the air in the basket. The French thought it was then safe enough for people to fly in the same way as the animals.

Because the hot air soon cooled, the first balloons could not stay in the air for a long time. A Frenchman then made a balloon out of varnished silk and filled it with gas. The gas was hydrogen which was lighter than air. A flight was made that lasted two hours carrying two men over Paris. From these early balloons in France came the idea of making larger airships.

Today ballooning is a sport. Races are held and you can even go for a joy-ride in a balloon. Hot air is now used to fill the canopy. A burner is carried on board to make this air whenever it is needed.

(1)   Besides a rooster, the other bird that went in a balloon was a ....

(2)   A .... was used to carry men in a balloon.

(3)   The first gas balloon was made out of ....

(4)   Two men flew over the city of .... in a gas balloon.

(5)   Large balloons are called ....

(6)   The gas used in early balloons was ....

(7)   In a modern balloon a .... makes hot air.

(8)   To take a fun flight is to go on a ....

        Write the words that mean:

(9)   secure ....   (10) less heavy ....

(11)   the opposite of 'late' ....

(12)   the opposite of 'heated' ....

Set 24   Crossword   (Spelling and Vocabulary)

Across
1 A hen goes '.....'.
3 part of a tree
5 opposite to 'ugly'
8 This bird flies at night.
9 One and ..... make two.
10 We all ..... water.
11 the early part of the day
13 A bee is a ..... insect.
14 They keep our feet warm.
15 Elephants are ..... animals.
19 Men and women ..... cars.
20 You ..... for things from shops.
21 A rat can be caught in a ..... .

Down
1 a baby tiger
2 It flies on the end of a string.
4 Fish can be caught in one.
5 A flower is a ..... .
6 A house has a back ..... .
7 Mum washes dishes in the ..... .
11 A hippo has a big ..... .
12 Rabbits live below the ..... .
13 short word for bicycle
16 not at home
17 twelve months
18 opposite to 'under'

Set 25   Animals   (Vocabulary)

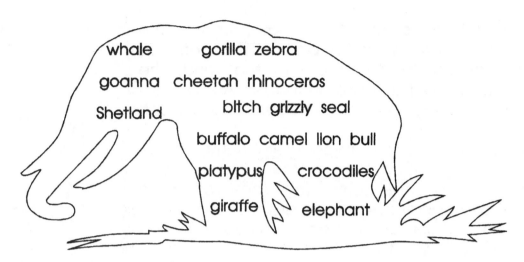

whale   gorilla zebra

goanna   cheetah rhinoceros

Shetland   bitch grizzly seal

buffalo camel lion bull

platypus   crocodiles

giraffe   elephant

(1)   The .... is heavy and has horns on its nose.

(2)   A .... is a large and powerful ape.

(3)   The .... is a striped animal like a horse.

(4)   The .... is an Australian reptile that climbs trees.

(5)   In some rivers of Australia there are man-eating ....

(6)   The animal known as the 'ship of the desert' is the ....

(7)   A .... is a female dog.

(8)   A .... is a male cow.

(9)   The .... is a large wild cat that is the fastest animal.

(10) A large Canadian bear is the ....

(11) The largest cat and king of beasts is the ....

(12) The world's largest animal that lives in the sea is the ....

(13) An animal once hunted by Red Indians is the ....

(14) The web-footed Australian .... has a duck's bill.

(15) The .... is the tallest animal in the world.

(16) The .... pony is very small but strong.

Set 26 The Ship of the Desert (Spelling in Context)

The camel is an animal that is at home in the desert. Deserts are dry sandy parts of the world. To stop this animal from sinking into the sand, the camel has soft spongy pads on its feet. A horse has hard hoofs and would perhaps become stuck in soft sand.

On the camel's back is a very useful hump. When making a long journey, the camel can use food which is stored in the hump. This does not mean that the camel carries grass or grain in its hump - the food has of course been eaten before travelling and then turned into fat.

Inside a camel's stomach there are pockets in which water can be stored. There is no need for it to drink very often. Arab men and women keep camels. They are used much as we use cars and trucks. But in a way they are better than cars because they give milk to drink and make cheese. They have hair that can be made into clothes. They can be killed for meat and leather made from their skins.

(1)   Camels live in dry parts of the world called ....

(2)   Pads prevent the camel from .... in the sand.

(3)   Horses' feet are called ....

(4)   Pockets store water in a camels ....

(5)   Some men and women who keep camels are called ....

(6)   Camel milk can be made into ....

(7)   Camel skin can be made into ....

(8)   Fat is stored in a camel's ....

Write the words that mean:

(9)   going down ....

(10) elastic ....

(11) the opposite of 'seldom' ....

(12) the opposite of 'worse' ....

Set 27   Crossword   (Spelling and Vocabulary)

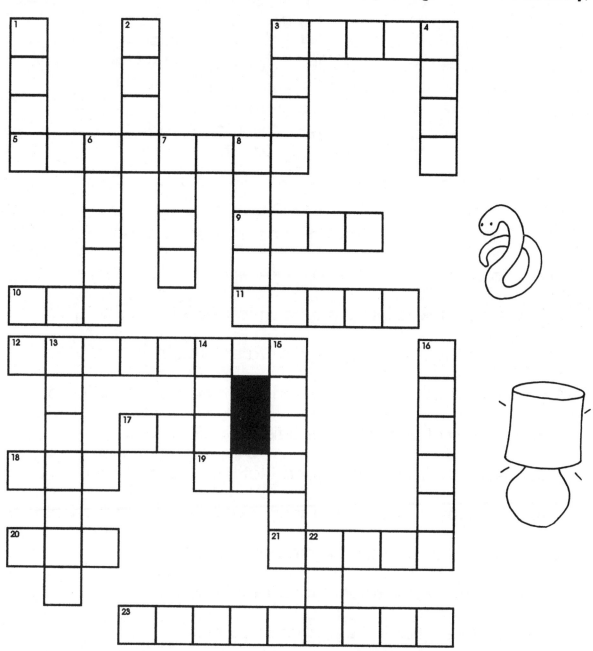

Across
1 The sun brings ..... to the world.
5 We like to have ..... parties.
9 You can skip with a ..... .
10 wet dirt
11 They live in soil and wriggle.
12 We keep dry with it in rain.
17 meat from a pig
18 an Australian tree
19 A meat ..... is covered with pastry.
20 more than one man
21 At a ..... we eat cakes.
23 December 25th.

Down
1 a baby sheep
2 A ..... keeps you warm.
3 a woman
4 Some parrots can ..... .
6 A tennis ball is ..... .
7 A house is a ..... .
8 A bow can shoot an ..... .
13 Sixty ..... make an hour.
14 a small table light
15 not awake
16 wanting food
22 drawing or painting

Set 28   Sea Creatures   (Vocabulary)

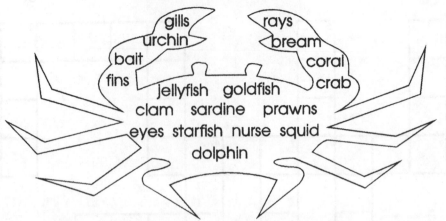

(1)   The .... is kept as a pet in a bowl or tank.

(2)   To catch fish you need a hook with .... on it.

(3)   A playful whale that has been tamed is the ....

(4)   A fish breathes oxygen from water through its ....

(5)   The .... is a small fish that is canned for us to eat.

(6)   Instead of arms and legs a fish has ....

(7)   A sea creature with nippers that lives in a shell is the ....

(8)   The grey .... is a shark that lives in Australian waters.

(9)   A creature with five pointed arms is a ....

(10)   A common fish caught for eating in Australia is the ....

(11)   The Great Barrier Reef is made up of ....

(12)   The giant .... with eight arms can attack a whale.

(13)   Shrimps and .... feed on dead things in the sea.

(14)   The sea .... is round and covered with spines.

(15)   The .... has no bones and can sting swimmers.

(16)   .... are fish that flap their wide fins like giant birds.

(17)   A .... is a very large seashell.

(18)   A fish cannot close its ....

Set 29   The First Machine   (Spelling in Context)

A machine helps us to do a job better. Without one we can only use our hands. A washing machine for example, helps us to wash better and faster than if we scrubbed by hand. It was a cave man or woman who first used a machine. A rock had to be moved. The person tried using bare hands. It was too heavy. Then taking a strong branch of a tree, he or she used the branch as a lever and the rock moved. The first machine was invented! Today we use a crowbar made of iron to lever things. We use two levers when we row a boat or cut with a pair of scissors. When children play on a seesaw they lift each other up and down quite easily as they are using a lever.

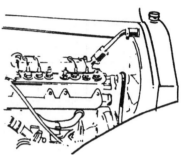

Another important invention was the wheel. This was another kind of machine that made it easier to lift things. A crane works with wheels. When used with an axle, the wheel made it easier to pull loads. This went a step farther when a steam engine was made to make wheels turn. Petrol and diesel engines followed. Cars and trains were born. Imagine what it was like before machines were used!

(1)   A lever is a kind of ....

(2)   Two levers are at work when we cut with ....

(3)   A modern lever made to move rocks is a ....

(4)   Children who play on a .... are using a lever.

(5)   A crane is an example of a machine that uses ....

(6)   The first engines were driven by ....

    Write the words that mean:

(7)   shifted ....

(8)   sturdy ....

(9)   task ....

(10) youngsters ....

(11) the opposite of 'harder' ....

(12) the opposite of 'slower' ....

Set 30　　Crossword　(Spelling and Vocabulary)

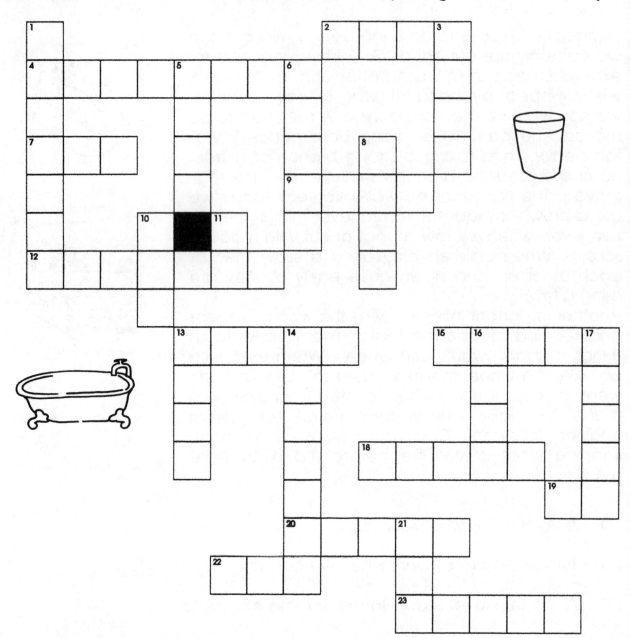

Across

2 A cow gives us ..... .
4 the day after today
7 We have ..... legs.
9 not fat
12 not anything
13 Coal is a ..... colour.
15 four less than seven
18 You ..... down a slippery dip.
19 I ride ..... bike.
20 opposite of the 'left' side
22 It opens a lock.
23 dollars and cents

Down

1 A train stops at one.
3 We must ..... all flies.
5 the top of a house
6 Snow is ..... in colour.
8 You use one eye to ..... .
10 Sue is tall and ..... is strong.
11 We put butter ..... bread.
13 We wash ourselves in it.
14 Australia is a large ..... .
16 Fingers are part of your ..... .
17 not late
21 edge of a dress or skirt

Answers to Basic Skills Spelling/Vocabulary Level 1 – Item No. 61

Set 1 (1) bootees (2) trunks (3) veil (4) jeans (5) sweater (6) pyjamas (7) uniform (8) rompers (9) bikini (10) thongs (11) petticoat (12) slippers (13) sneakers (14) sandal (15) gloves

Set 2 (1) dark (2) larger (3) hooting (4) dead (5) claws (6) seven (7) mice, frogs, insects

Set 3 **Across** 1 house 3 broom 5 tent 7 sea 9 six 10 tug 12 hat 14 bus 15 early 16 bee 18 happy 20 legs 22 girl
Down 1 hot 2 sit 4 mice 6 nest 8 axe 11 up 13 teeth 14 bone 16 ball 17 egg 19 pig 21 so

Set 4 (1) tart (2) coffee (3) butter (4) hamburger (5) rice (6) tuna (7) tomato (8) ginger (9) squash (10) carrot (11) yoghurt (12) crumpets (13) rump (14) sausage (15) lemonade

Set 5 (1) pirates (2) people (3) skull (4) lonely (5) hidden (6) daggers (7) black (8) Navy (9) hanged (10) gold, silver, jewels

Set 6 **Across** 1 puppy 3 pocket 6 lion 7 bell 8 water 11 odd 12 fences 14 pond 16 go 20 dear 21 rake
Down 2 yellow 4 kind 5 teacher 7 bird 9 tap 10 rat 12 frog 13 cap 15 door 17 old 18 trot 19 bed 22 and

Set 7 (1) cry (2) stroll (3) stack (4) relax (5) slide (6) repair (7) tumble (8) worry (9) construct (10) reason (11) tiptoe (12) raise (13) prepare (14) approach (15) decide (16) bustle (17) haul (18) shove (19) choose (20) forget

Set 8 (1) Africa (2) metres (3) patchy (4) tufted (5) lions (6) luckily (7) nearly (8) watch (9) hard

Set 9 **Across** 1 rain 3 week 4 tin 5 garden 10 shoes 11 calf 13 bread 15 in 17 horse 20 grass 21 pencil
Down 1 ring 2 pet 4 tall 6 rock 7 nose 8 his 9 mop 11 cup 12 fish 14 dress 16 peg 18 open 19 bag

Set 10 (1) title (2) author (3) drawings (4) hero (5) wizard (6) villain (7) pixie (8) mystery (9) dragon (10) genie (11) giant (12) textbook (13) cartoonist (14) wand (15) legend (16) spooky (17) heroine

Set 11 (1) cats (2) trees (3) spots, leaves (4) tiger (5) skins (6) coats (7) trying (8) monkeys (9) large (10) spring (11) **cunning** (12) hard

Set 12 **Across** 1 ant 5 flower 7 pony 8 elephant 12 gate 13 night 14 woman 16 river 18 dolls 20 milkman 23 smack 24 kid 25 ears
Down 1 apple 2 tan 3 often 4 dog 6 rabbit 9 log 10 pat 11 ten 14 windows 15 bricks 17 red 19 smoke 21 nail 22 pan

Set 13 (1) igloo (2) unit (3) wigwam (4) cottage (5) mansion (6) sampan (7) terrace-house (8) garage (9) church (10) hospital (11) palace (12) motel (13) penthouse (14) factory (15) cinema (16) chalet (17) caravan (18) duplex

Set 14 (1) saying (2) lying (3) eat (4) thin (5) roof (6) dog (7) gate (8) crept (9) spotted (10) tricked (11) returned

Set 15 **Across** 1 grandmother 5 cake 7 dim 8 see 9 nut 11 policeman 12 breakfast 16 yes 19 road 20 funny 21 jet
Down 1 good 2 animal 3 duck 4 engine 6 even 8 sell 10 town 12 baby 13 flag 14 tiger 15 gold 17 soft 18 eyes

Set 16 (1) bell (2) exercise (3) chalk (4) principal (5) dictionary (6) biro (7) paints (8) projector (9) mathematics (10) desks (11) pupils (12) rubber (13) library (14) carnival (15) playground (16) atlas (17) globe (18) teacher

Set 17 (1) planets (2) telescopes (3) black (4) space-ship (5) rocket (6) gravity (7) float (8) Venus (9) ends (10) burning (11) inside (12) cannot

Set 18 **Across** 2 outside 5 boat 6 cut 7 listen 9 meat 11 God 12 skip 13 feather 15 sad 16 and 18 feed 20 new 21 pick 23 planes

Down 1 cab 2 orange 3 shell 4 burns 8 sick 9 mug 10 add 13 fire 14 honey 15 seven 17 always 19 dark 22 in

Set 19 (1) station (2) cattle (3) shearer (4) dairy (5) poultry (6) orchard (7) plough (8) combine (9) grazier (10) gardener (11) stable (12) trough (13) tractor (14) fences (15) bales (16) hay

Set 20 (1) snow (2) ground (3) fur (4) boots (5) cold (6) blocks (7) oil (8) usually (9) enter (10) back (11) warm (12) often

Set 21 **Across** 2 church 4 glad 6 clap 7 wheels 10 ram 11 skate 12 grandfather 17 we 18 noise 21 almost 23 splash

Down 1 jug 2 city 3 happy 5 dishes 8 lit 9 paw 12 green 13 arm 14 fat 15 horn 16 races 19 ice 20 eats 22 melt

Set 22 (1) goods (2) taxi (3) helicopter (4) balloon (5) cycle (6) guard (7) runway (8) seaplane (9) airport (10) truck (11) express (12) tower (13) tunnel (14) engine (15) signal (16) carriage (17) coach (18) cockpit

Set 23 (1) duck (2) basket (3) silk (4) Paris (5) airships (6) hydrogen (7) burner (8) joy-ride (9) safe (10) lighter (11) early (12) cooled

Set 24 **Across** 1 cluck 3 branch 5 pretty 8 owl 9 one 10 drink 11 morning 13 busy 14 socks 15 heavy 19 drive 20 pay 21 trap

Down 1 cub 2 kite 4 net 5 plant 6 yard 7 sink 11 mouth 12 ground 13 bike 16 away 17 year 18 over

Set 25 (1) rhinoceros (2) gorilla (3) zebra (4) goanna (5) crocodiles (6) camel (7) bitch (8) bull (9) cheetah (10) grizzly (11) lion (12) whale (13) buffalo (14) platypus (15) giraffe (16) Shetland

Set 26 (1) deserts (2) sinking (3) hoofs (4) stomach (5) Arab (6) cheese (7) leather (8) hump (9) sinking (10) spongy (11) often (12) better

Set 27 **Across** 3 light 5 birthday 9 rope 10 mud 11 worms 12 umbrella 17 ham 18 gum 19 pie 20 men 21 party 23 Christmas

Down 1 lamb 2 coat 3 lady 4 talk 6 round 7 home 8 arrow 13 minutes 14 lamp 15 asleep 16 hungry 22 art

Set 28 (1) goldfish (2) bait (3) dolphin (4) gills (5) sardine (6) fins (7) crab (8) nurse (9) starfish (10) bream (11) coral (12) squid (13) prawns (14) urchin (15) jellyfish (16) rays (17) clam (18) eyes

Set 29 (1) machine (2) scissors (3) crowbar (4) seesaw (5) wheels (6) steam (7) moved (8) strong (9) job (10) children (11) easier (12) faster

Set 30 **Across** 2 milk 4 tomorrow 7 two 9 thin 12 nothing 13 black 15 three 18 slide 19 my 20 right 22 key 23 money

Down 1 station 3 kill 5 roof 6 white 8 wink 10 she 11 on 13 bath 14 country 16 hand 17 early 21 hem

Set 31 (1) boring (2) brave (3) muscular (4) podgy (5) honest (6) slender (7) jolly (8) clumsy (9) lame (10) lazy (11) active (12) friendly (13) wise (14) shy (15) talkative (16) gloomy (17) weary (18) modest

Set 32 (1) farmers (2) shearer (3) fleece (4) Sydney (5) washed (6) yarn (7) kilograms (8) sweat (9) dirty (10) nearly (11) summer (12) loaded

Set 33 **Across** 1 sip 2 find 4 old 6 wolf 8 rod 11 rug 12 pup 13 bear 15 shut 16 big 18 deer 21 tan 23 today 24 stop

Down 1 snow 2 fin 3 down 5 dry 7 fog 9 deep 10 pump 11 rip 13 bring 14 rib 15 short 17 God 19 toe 20 lad 22 nap

Set 34 (1) porthole (2) dinghy (3) port (4) lifeboat (5) radar (6) anchor (7) cabin (8) yacht (9) ferry (10) oars (11) rigging (12) liner (13) funnel (14) decks (15) compass (16) railings (17) bunk

Set 35 (1) tastes (2) chicle (3) juice (4) jungles (5) oozes (6) strawberry (7) machines (8) taste (9) while (10) bucket (11) world (12) thick

Set 36 **Across** 1 blue 3 pips 4 why 6 kitten 9 store 11 pit 12 been 13 dinner 15 paper 17 do 19 wag 21 bin 23 web 24 each

Down 1 begin 2 us 3 park 5 hear 7 ill 8 top 10 tub 13 draw 14 read 15 please 16 end 18 own 20 games 22 act

Set 37 (1) spiderling (2) butterfly (3) locust (4) thread (5) moth (6) ladybird (7) colony (8) fly (9) cicada (10) blowfly (11) redback (12) pollen (13) abdomen (14) wasp (15) funnel-web (16) caterpillars

Set 38 (1) harbour (2) tyres (3) barges (4) sideways (5) message (6) cable (7) metal (8) powerful (9) pushing (10) needed (11) pieces (12) arrive

Set 39 **Across** 2 farmer 6 march 8 mix 9 ride 11 you 13 story 14 cow 16 wash 18 high 20 mat 21 near 25 goat 26 dance

Down 1 hard 3 monkey 4 room 5 box 7 hurry 10 cot 12 use 14 cooking 15 where 17 hut 19 gone 22 rob 23 hole 24 gun

Set 40 (1) bowler (2) serve (3) fielder (4) pitch (5) court (6) wicket-keeper (7) lob (8) batsman (9) return (10) boundary (11) slips (12) smash (13) pads (14) umpire (15) catch (16) century

Set 41 (1) Plants (2) wrapped (3) knife (4) pictures (5) people (6) arrow (7) careful (8) plenty (9) besides (10) path (11) tough (12) short

Set 42 **Across** 1 their 3 bad 5 left 6 shines 9 cat 10 mouse 12 much 15 neck **16 poor** 19 name 20 tie 22 hop 23 foot 24 smile

Down 2 roots 3 bottom 4 pin 5 lunch 7 hum 8 east 11 of 13 red 14 skin 16 pen 17 out 18 help 21 into 22 ham

Set 43 (1) typist (2) artist (3) tailor (4) **pharmacist** (5) jockey (6) carpenter (7) clown (8) detective (9) plumber (10) librarian (11) matron (12) miner (13) mechanic (14) cobbler (15) conductor (16) dentist (17) juggler (18) florist

Set 44 (1) eleven (2) soldiers (3) English (4) build (5) fired (6) farmers (7) gold (8) prisons (9) money (10) houses (11) began (12) raised

Set 45 **Across** 1 shakes 3 state 6 thank 8 part 9 climb 11 lay 12 best 13 swim 15 tail 18 dim 20 stay 22 very 24 side 25 small

Down 1 sob 2 after 4 talk 5 tins 7 knock 8 pal 10 bit 14 wood 15 they 16 lot 17 fly 19 move 21 nip 23 rim

Set 46 (1) brain (2) heart (3) throat (4) skeleton (5) joints (6) muscles (7) ankle (8) tongue,mouth (9) blood (10) beard (11) eyelash (12) nostrils (13) limbs (14) skull (15) nerves (16) pores (17) stomach

Set 47 (1) bubbles (2) syrup (3) mountains (4) active (5) town (6) buildings (7) cooling (8) hard (9) crack (10) suddenly (11) town (12) again

Answers to Basic Skills Spelling/Vocabulary Level 1 – Item No. 61

Set 48 **Across** 2 war 4 fresh 6 who 8 cent 9 tug 10 toes 11 now 12 front 13 again 16 blows 18 bark 21 rum 22 drop 24 pod 25 paint

Down 1 is 2 worse 3 rock 5 hog 6 write 7 any 9 tow 11 net 13 afraid 14 ask 15 nod 17 seed 19 almost 20 keep 23 pep

Set 49 (1) barking (2) buzzing (3) beating (4) squealing (5) quacking (6) purring (7) chirping (8) tooting (9) neighing (10) trumpeting (11) pealing (12) booming (13) crowing (14) slamming (15) jingling (16) pinging (17) squeaking (18) crunching

Set 50 (1) bulldog (2) pincers (3) needle (4) stones (5) recognised (6) soldiers (7) powerful (8) heavier (9) rear (10) inject (11) beware (12) scurrying

Set 51 **Across** 1 food 4 cop 5 mail 6 last 8 sap 10 smell 11 bakers 13 long 15 shop 16 town 17 run 19 elf 20 finish 21 dam

Down 1 fields 2 on 3 ape 4 close 5 mill 7 time 9 pads 12 aunt 13 lop 14 bank 15 sniff 17 rush 18 band 19 elm

Set 52 (1) newsagent (2) hairdresser (3) boutique (4) hardware (5) sports (6) delicatessen (7) hobby (8) camera (9) butcher (10) bakery (11) supermarket (12) escalator (13) counter (14) cafe (15) mirror (16) cleaner (17) record

Set 53 (1) birds (2) pairs (3) melted (4) island (5) chickens (6) wall (7) wanted (8) strapping (9) earlier (10) unluckily (11) really (12) jumped

Set 54 **Across** 1 paid 3 make 5 start 7 push 8 cold 10 jog 11 mad 12 many 14 bright 16 gap 18 toys 21 tree 22 try 24 seal

Down 1 Pam 2 die 4 alone 5 sheep 6 tag 9 drum 10 Jim 13 always 14 beg 15 hit 17 post 19 stars 20 set 23 map

Set 55 (1) satellite (2) galaxy (3) astronaut (4) rocket (5) countdown (6) meteor (7) orbit (8) planet (9) blast-off (10) tracking (11) capsule (12) lift-off (13) cosmic (14) docking (15) module (16) launching (17) re-enter (18) space

Set 56 (1) bones (2) penguin (3) stomachs (4) sandpaper (5) beaches (6) harbours (7) true (8) instead (9) devour (10) chance (11) dangerous (12) savage

Set 57 **Across** 1 waves 4 fox 5 flat 6 on 7 days 9 eggs 11 grip 12 cars 16 up 17 snail 20 wet 21 train 22 mother 25 few

Down 1 wear 2 send 3 ox 4 flying 5 face 8 tape 10 get 12 count 13 chew 14 butter 15 wig 18 nun 19 mask 23 off 24 how

Set 58 (1) swamp (2) volcano (3) plain (4) valley (5) forest (6) rapids (7) lake (8) desert (9) channel (10) island (11) coast (12) cliff (13) stream (14) equator (15) meadow (16) mountain (17) iceberg (18) spring

Set 59 (1) flowers (2) sunlight (3) water (4) thistle (5) animals (6) fruits (7) ocean (8) hooks (9) close (10) float (11) little (12) soil

Set 60 **Across** 1 jam 2 caught 4 roars 7 crumb 9 old 10 one 11 grey 13 plates 15 jump 19 on 20 pram 21 none 22 ink 23 dip 24 child

Down 1 jar 3 hard 5 own 6 sing 7 clay 8 mane 12 rot 14 fun 15 job 16 pink 17 van 18 damp 20 peach 23 Dad

Set 31   Kinds of People   (Vocabulary)

talkative   shy   boring

modest   brave   podgy

muscular   slender   lazy

clumsy   wise   honest

gloomy   friendly   lame

weary   active   jolly

(1)   A .... person tires us with his or her talking.

(2)   A .... person is not afraid .

(3)   A .... person is very strong.

(4)   A .... person is rather fat.

(5)   An .... person does not steal or tell lies.

(6)   A .... person is not fat.

(7)   A .... person is always smiling and happy.

(8)   A .... person always drops or knocks things over.

(9)   A .... person has something wrong with his or her leg.

(10)   A .... person does not like work.

(11)   An .... person is always busy doing something.

(12)   A .... person is always ready to help and be kind.

(13)   A .... person does not do or say silly things.

(14)   A .... person does not like meeting strangers.

(15)   A .... person never seems to stop talking.

(16)   A .... person nevers smiles and always feels sad.

(17)   A .... person always seems to be tired.

(18)   A .... person does not boast and does not show off.

Set 32 Wool (Spelling in Context)

Wool is soft hair from the coat of sheep and goats. People wear woollen clothes to keep them warm in winter and cool in summer. Wool is able to protect your skin from changes in the weather. It is not too heavy when it is cold, and when you sweat in the summer the wool does not feel wet.

In Australia we have many sheep, and farmers make money by selling the wool. Once a year a shearer comes to cut off the wool which is packed in bags called 'bales'. The shearing from a fully grown sheep is called a 'fleece'. Dirty parts of the fleece are cut off in the shearing shed. A good fleece weighs about twelve kilograms.

The wool is pressed flat so that it does not take up too much space. It is then sent by road or rail to ports. Sydney is a large port where ships are loaded with bales for countries like England, China and Japan.

Wool has to be washed with soap and water in large vats. It is then spun into yarn which looks like fluffy string. It is now ready to be woven into cloth. A long woman's coat will need nearly two kilograms of raw wool to make.

(1)   Wool in Australia is produced by ....

(2)   A .... cuts the wool from sheep.

(3)   Wool from a fully grown sheep is called a ....

(4)   The port mentioned in the passage is ....

(5)   Before spinning wool it has to be ....

(6)   Wool that is ready for weaving is called ....

(7)   A woman's coat needs nearly two .... of wool.

       Write each word that means:

(8)   perspire ....   (9)   unclean ....

(10) almost ....   (11) the opposite of 'winter' ....

(12) the opposite of 'unloaded' ....

Set 33 Crossword (Spelling and Vocabulary)

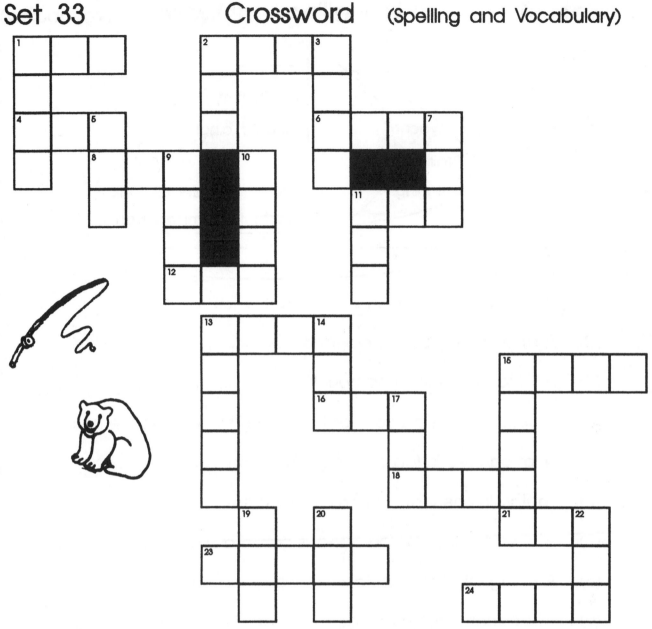

Across
1 drink slowly
2 I will try to ..... the lost pen.
4 not young
6 a wild animal like a dog
8 You can fish with it.
11 a thick mat
12 a baby dog
13 a big furry animal
15 closed
16 large
18 animal with horns
21 a light brown colour
23 this day
24 halt

Down
1 It is cold, soft and white
2 part of a fish
3 not up
5 not wet
7 a kind of mist
9 opposite to 'shallow'
10 We ..... up tyres.
11 to tear
13 fetch
14 chest bone
15 not long
17 We pray to ..... .
19 part of your foot
20 another name for 'boy'
22 a short sleep

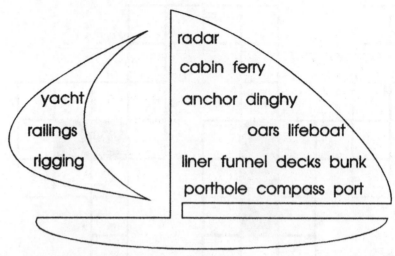

(1)   A window aboard a ship is called a ....

(2)   A small rowing boat is called a ....

(3)   Another name for a harbour is a ....

(4)   A .... is a small boat carried on a ship to save lives.

(5)   Ships can see in fog or at night by using ....

(6)   To stop in one place at sea a ship uses an ....

(7)   A room for sleeping on a ship is called a ....

(8)   A sailing ship that can take part in races is a ....

(9)   A ship that takes passengers for short distances is a ....

(10) A rowing boat is moved by using a pair of ....

(11) The ropes and tackle of a sailing ship are known as ....

(12) A .... is a large ship that carries passengers overseas.

(13) Smoke comes out from a .... on a ship.

(14) We can walk around on .... aboard a ship.

(15) Sailors can find their way at sea by using a ....

(16) To stop people falling overboard a ship has ....

(17) A bed on board ship is called a ....

Chewing Gum (Spelling in Context)

Do you like to chew gum? At first it tastes sweet. Then after chewing for a while the taste goes away. You have swallowed all the sugar and flavouring that was added to the gum. In fact all that you will have left in your mouth will be the chicle.

Chicle grows in Mexico and nearby countries. It is made by boiling down the milky juice from the sapodilla tree. This tree grows in hot jungles. A worker makes a cut in the trunk and the milky juice oozes out into a bucket. The juice is cooked in pots and made into cakes of chicle. These cakes are thick and sticky. Millions of kilograms are sent all over the world.

In Australia and other countries that make chewing gum, the chicle is treated by adding softeners, sweeteners and flavouring such as mint or strawberry. All the work is done in machines which wrap the finished sticks or pellets of gum.

(1)   When you first chew gum it .... sweet.

(2)   The basic part of chewing gum is called ....

(3)   The .... of a sapodilla tree is used in making gum.

(4)   Sapodilla trees together grow in hot ....

(5)   Juice .... out from cuts in the tree.

(6)   Mint and .... are two flavours mentioned.

(7)   Chewing gum is made and wrapped with the help of ....

   Write the words that mean:

(8)   flavour ....

(9)   time ....

(10) pail ....

(11) globe ....

(12) the opposite of 'thin' ....

Set 36   Crossword   (Spelling and Vocabulary)

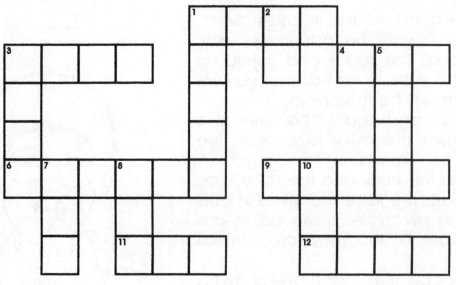

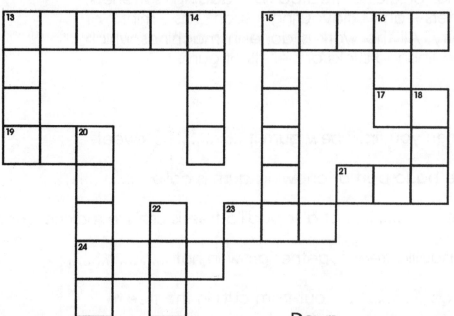

Across

1   The sky on a hot day is ..... .
3   Apples and oranges have ..... .
4   A question can ask ..... .
6   a baby cat
9   a large shop
11   a deep wide hole
12   I have ..... to the beach this morning.
13   We eat ..... at night.
15   We get news from the ..... .
17   ..... you like lollies?
19   Dogs ..... their tails.
21   It holds rubbish.
23   a spider's home
24   Plums cost 10 cents ..... .

Down

1   start
2   Teacher set ..... work.
3   It has trees and swings.
5   You ..... with your ears.
7   not well
8   opposite to 'bottom'
10   Mum has a laundry ..... .
13   We ..... pictures.
14   I like to ..... books.
15   We must say ..... and thanks.
16   opposite of 'beginning'
18   to have
20   Cricket and football are ..... .
22   You can ..... in a play.

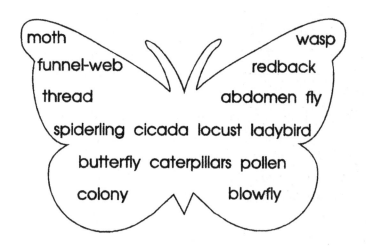

moth
funnel-web
thread
spiderling cicada locust ladybird
butterfly caterpillars pollen
colony
wasp
redback
abdomen fly
blowfly

(1)   A baby spider is called a ....

(2)   A .... is coloured and its wings fold upwards.

(3)   A .... is a pest that swarms and eats all kinds of plants.

(4)   Spiders spin their webs with fine ....

(5)   The brownish .... flies at night, and its wings fold flat.

(6)   The .... is a helpful insect that eats plant pests.

(7)   Ants are insects that live together in a ....

(8)   The common house .... leaves germs wherever it walks.

(9)   The .... sings in gum trees during the hot summer.

(10   The .... lays eggs that turn into maggots.

(11) The .... spider with a red stripe is poisonous.

(12) Bees carry .... from flower to flower.

(13) The stomach of an insect is called the ....

(14) A .... is an insect that can give you a nasty sting.

(15) The .... spider is brown or black and can kill you.

(16) Eggs of moths and butterflies hatch and become ....

Set 38   Tugboats   (Spelling in Context)

Tugboats, we call them tugs, are powerful little boats that are used to push and pull ships that have to tie up in ports or harbours. Thick ropes or old car tyres on the front or the sides of tugs act like bumper bars. Without these, tugs would dent or scrape the paint off ships that were being pushed. It sometimes takes as many as three tugs pushing together to move a large liner sideways.

Tugs have other jobs to do. They pull long flat boats called barges that often have no engines of their own. Barges carry things that are needed around the harbour. Some ships have trouble at sea. If a ship's engines break down the captain sends a radio message for help. A tug is sent out to tow the ship back to port. A strong steel cable is used for pulling, as rough seas could break even the strongest rope.

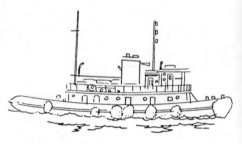

Old ships that are no longer fit to be used are sold for scrap metal. It is often the job of one or two tugs to pull them to places like Hong Kong and Singapore. When they arrive, many workers cut them up into pieces which are melted down.

(1)   Another name for a port is a ....

(2)   Ropes or car .... are used to stop tugs denting ships.

(3)   Flat .... are boats that may have no engines.

(4)   When a liner has to be moved .... it can take three tugs to do the job.

(5)   A radio .... lets people know a ship is in trouble.

(6)   A steel .... is needed by a tug pulling a ship at sea.

(7)   An old ship is cut up for its scrap ....

       Write the words that mean:

(8)   strong ....   (9)   shoving ....

(10) wanted ....   (11) bits ....

(12) the opposite of 'leave' ....

Set 39   Crossword   (Spelling and Vocabulary)

Across
2   He keeps cattle or grows crops.
6   When soldiers ..... they walk in step.
8   stir together
9   We ..... horses.
11   ..... are reading this.
13   a tale
14   It gives us milk.
16   We use soap to ..... .
18   opposite to 'low'
20   a small rug
21   close by
25   animal with horns and beard
26   move to music

Down
1   opposite to 'soft'
3   animal that looks like us
4   It has four walls
5   a ..... of matches
7   We go fast when we are in a ..... .
10   Baby sleeps in it.
12   We ..... spoons to eat ice cream.
14   Mum is ..... the dinner.
15   in what place?
17   a little house
19   He has ..... away.
22   to steal
23   You can dig one with a spade.
24   You can shoot with one.

Set 40   Cricket and Tennis   (Vocabulary)

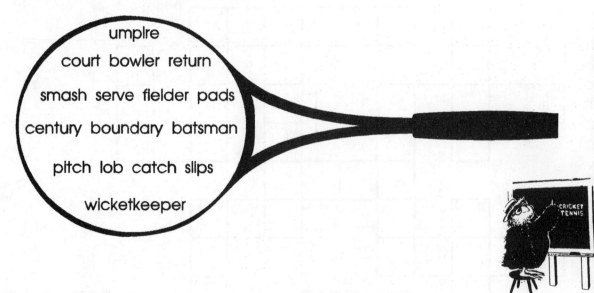

umpire
court bowler return
smash serve fielder pads
century boundary batsman
pitch lob catch slips
wicketkeeper

(1)   The .... tries to get the batsman out at cricket.

(2)   You .... a tennis ball to begin the game.

(3)   A .... in cricket tries to catch the ball with bare hands.

(4)   The game of cricket is played on a ....

(5)   The game of tennis is played on a ....

(6)   The .... has gloves and stands behind the wicket.

(7)   To .... in tennis is to hit the ball over someone's head.

(8)   In cricket the .... hopes to score as many runs as possible.

(9)   After a ball is served in tennis a person has to .... it.

(10) A cricket ball hit over or past the .... scores 6 or 4.

(11) .... fielders are grouped together near the batsman.

(12) To hit the ball hard and downwards at tennis is to ....it.

(13) A batsman wears .... to protect his legs.

(14) An .... is in charge of play in both tennis and cricket.

(15) In cricket you try to .... a ball hit by a batsman.

(16) To make a .... in cricket you must score a hundred.

Set 41   The Jungles (Spelling In Context)

Jungles grow where it is hot and there is plenty of rain. Sun and water make plants and trees grow tall. Besides trees, jungles have long vines that hang down or are wrapped around tree trunks.

The floor of the jungle is often thick with plants. A person walking through the jungle often needs a machete to cut a path through the plants which we call 'undergrowth'. A machete is a large knife like a short sword that is used to slash thin branches or tough grass.

The largest jungles in the world are in South America. The mighty Amazon River flows through hundreds of kilometres of jungle. Perhaps you have seen pictures on television of the Indian people who live there. These Indians hunt animals with bows and arrows or blow-guns. A favourite dish is roast monkey! They fish in the Amazon River, but have to be careful of small pirahna fish which can attack in large numbers if they scent a cut in the skin.

(1) .... and trees grow when there is sun and rain.

(2) Vines can be seen hanging or .... round tree trunks.

(3) A machete is a large .... used to cut undergrowth.

(4) On television it is possible to see .... of jungles.

(5) Native .... who live near the Amazon are called Indians.

(6) An Indian may hunt with a blow-gun or a bow and ....

(7) Indians must be .... of pirahna fish when swimming.

Write the words that mean:

(8) lots ....

(9) as well as ....

(10) trail ....

(11) strong ....

(12) the opposite of 'long' ....

Set 42   Crossword   (Spelling and Vocabulary)

Across
1. belonging to them
3. not good
5. opposite to 'right' side
6. The sun ..... on you.
9. a kind of pet
10. It hates cats.
12. I haven't ..... money left.
15. Your head sits on it.
16. having little or no money
19. His ..... is Jim.
20. worn by men around the neck
22. You can ..... on one leg.
23. A shoe goes on it.
24. Happy people ..... .

Down
2. Plants have them in the ground.
3. opposite to 'top'
4. It is sharp and can prick.
5. food at midday
7. You ..... a tune with mouth shut.
8. opposite to 'west'
11. a cup ..... tea
13. Lips are a ..... colour.
14. It covers your body.
16. You write with it.
17. not in
18. To aid is to ..... .
21. Kick the ball ..... the net.
22. meat from a pig

Set 43   Jobs People Do   (Vocabulary)

> pharmacist artist clown carpenter dentist typist jockey mechanic
> tailor cobbler conductor matron detective miner plumber librarian

(1)   A .... works in an office and types letters.

(2)   An .... paints or draws pictures.

(3)   A .... measures then makes suits or clothes for you.

(4)   A .... has a shop where he or she makes up medicines.

(5)   A .... rides a horse in a race.

(6)   A .... builds the wooden parts of a house.

(7)   A .... works in a circus and makes you laugh.

(8)   A .... is a policeman who tries to solve crimes.

(9)   A .... repairs or puts pipes and taps in houses.

(10) A .... is in charge of a library where you find books.

(11) A .... is in charge of nurses at a hospital.

(12) A .... digs for coal or other minerals.

(13) A .... repairs motor cars or other machines.

(14) A .... repairs shoes that are worn.

(15) A .... collects fares on a train or bus.

(16) A .... works on your teeth.

(17) A (purser ganger juggler) .... performs tricks.

(18) A (furrier florist farrier) .... sells flowers.

Set 44　　How Australia Began　(Spelling in Context)

Arthur Phillip brought the first white people to Australia.

He sailed from England in 1787 with eleven ships filled with convicts. The convicts were taken from the prisons which were overcrowded. Among the convicts were men and women who had stolen small amounts of money or even food. Also on board the ships were soldiers to guard these people.

On January 26th, 1788 he arrived at Sydney Cove. The English flag was raised. Guns were fired as a salute, and Phillip claimed the land for the King of England. The convicts set to work to build the city of Sydney. They made roads, bridges and houses. Many of the convict stone buildings are standing today.

Then came the time when England stopped sending any more convicts to Australia. Instead, free settlers arrived to become farmers and workers in the towns. In 1851 many thousands of people arrived to dig for gold which had been found near Bathurst. January 26th is Australia Day. It all began over 200 years ago.

(1)　Phillip sailed with .... ships full of convicts.

(2)　On the ships .... guarded the convicts.

(3)　Phillip had the .... flag raised at Sydney Cove.

(4)　Convicts worked to .... stone buildings.

(5)　Phillip .... guns as a salute on January 26th.

(6)　Later settlers became workers or ....

(7)　In 1851 people came to Australia looking for ....

Write the words that mean:

(8)　jails ....　　　(9)　cash ....

(10) homes ....　　(11) started ....

(12) the opposite of 'lowered' ....

Set 45

Crossword (Spelling and Vocabulary)

Across
1 I like chocolate milk ..... .
3 The ..... of New South Wales.
6 Say please and ..... you.
8 less than the whole of something
9 go up
11 Hens ..... eggs.
12 nothing better
13 A fish can ..... in water.
15 A dog can wag it.
18 A light that is not bright is ..... .
20 not move
22 The sun is ..... hot.
24 The ..... of a square is straight.
25 not big

Down
1 to cry quietly
2 opposite of 'before'
4 speak
5 Beans come in ..... .
7 You ..... on doors.
8 a friend
10 a little piece
14 It comes from trees.
15 ..... have a new car.
16 much
17 a dirty insect
19 go
21 A crab can ..... your toe.
23 A cup has one.

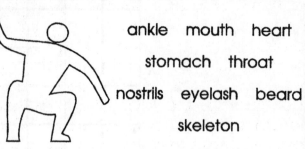

tongue brain pores   ankle mouth heart

muscles limbs   stomach throat

skull nerves joints   nostrils eyelash beard

blood   skeleton

(1)   The .... is the part of your body that does the thinking.

(2)   Your .... beats and acts as a pump for the blood.

(3)   Air and food passes down your ....

(4)   All the bones of the body make up the ....

(5)   Many of your bones move at the ....

(6)   To make the bones move we have many .... in the body.

(7)   The part where your foot joins the leg is the ....

(8)   Your .... which is in the .... helps you talk.

(9)   Your .... carries food to cells and is pumped by the heart.

(10) Hair on a man's face is called a ....

(11) A hair above or below the eye is called an ....

(12) The holes in your nose are called ....

(13) A word used for arms or legs is ....

(14) Your brain is protected by bones which form the ....

(15) You feel pain through the .... in your body.

(16) Sweat comes out from your skin through tiny ....

(17) Food goes down to the .... to be used by the body.

Set 47   Volcanoes   (Spelling in Context)

Deep down in the earth the rock is very hot. It is so hot that it boils and bubbles like toffee being made in a pan on a hot stove. Sometimes this hot rock pushes up through a crack in the earth. Up, up it comes, until it pours out on to the ground. This hot rock, called lava, is a fiery red and flows like syrup. After cooling, the lava becomes hard and blocks the crack in the earth. When more hot lava comes again it pushes through the cold lava and gradually a hill of lava is formed. This goes on for thousands of years until the hill becomes a mountain. We call mountains like this 'volcanoes'.

Australia has many old volcanoes. They have not been active for a long time and never will be. But some volcanoes keep sending out fire, smoke or lava from time to time. One volcano - Mount Vesuvius, in Italy, suddenly sent lava and ash down over a town called Pompeii. Many people died and buildings lay buried for hundreds of years until the town was uncovered.

(1) Hot rock deep down in the earth boils and ....

(2) When lava is hot it flows like .... or toffee.

(3) Hills of lava slowly grow into .... called volcanoes.

(4) An .... volcano is one that sends out ash, smoke or lava.

(5) Pompeii was a .... in Italy.

(6) The .... of Pompeii were buried for many years.

    Write each word that means:

(7) becoming cold ....

(8) solid ....

(9) chink ....

(10) all of a sudden ....

(11) city ....

(12) once more ....

Set 48   Crossword   (Spelling and Vocabulary)

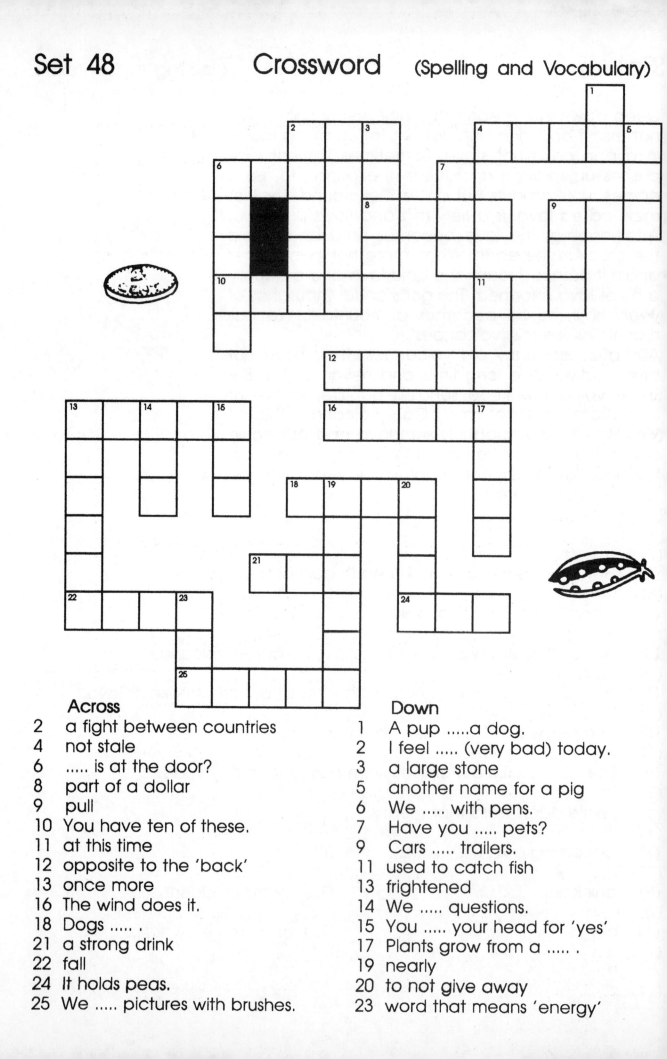

Across
2 a fight between countries
4 not stale
6 ..... is at the door?
8 part of a dollar
9 pull
10 You have ten of these.
11 at this time
12 opposite to the 'back'
13 once more
16 The wind does it.
18 Dogs ..... .
21 a strong drink
22 fall
24 It holds peas.
25 We ..... pictures with brushes.

Down
1 A pup .....a dog.
2 I feel ..... (very bad) today.
3 a large stone
5 another name for a pig
6 We ..... with pens.
7 Have you ..... pets?
9 Cars ..... trailers.
11 used to catch fish
13 frightened
14 We ..... questions.
15 You ..... your head for 'yes'
17 Plants grow from a ..... .
19 nearly
20 to not give away
23 word that means 'energy'

Set 49   Sounds   (Vocabulary)

> pinging booming beating purring barking squealing
> quacking chirping tooting neighing crunching trumpeting
> crowing slamming pealing squeaking buzzing jingling

(1) The dog was .... at the strange man.

(2) Bees were .... among the flowers.

(3) The explorer heard drums .... in the jungle.

(4) When we chased the baby pigs they began ....

(5) We could hear the ducks .... by the dam.

(6) My kitten is .... as she sits by the fire.

(7) Did you hear the sparrows .... this morning?

(8) In the city you often hear car horns ....

(9) A horse was .... in the paddock.

(10) During the film we heard elephants ....

(11) In the valley we heard church bells ....

(12) The .... of ship's guns at sea sounded like thunder.

(13) The .... of a rooster woke us up early.

(14) Our friends had arrived as we heard car doors ....

(15) The coins were .... in Robert's pocket.

(16) Bullets were .... during the fight between cowboys.

(17) A mouse makes a .... noise.

(18) Mary's footsteps came .... up the gravel driveway.

Set 50   Bulldog Ants   (Spelling in Context)

Bulldog ants live in Australia. Some people call them bullants for short. They have been given their name because they have very strong jaws like a bulldog. These ants are powerful for they can lift things that are much heavier than themselves. Not only can they bite with their jaws or pincers, but these ants have a sharp stinger at the rear of their bodies. The stinger is very like a needle that is used by a doctor. An ant is able to inject a kind of acid into the skin of a victim. The sting becomes extremely painful and swells into a large lump.

Bullants are easily recognised because they are larger than most other ants. They make nests under stones or fallen logs. Sometimes they make a mound on the ground, and you can see them scurrying around. These ants are hunters and do not fear other insects that are larger than themselves. They work together and attack like soldiers. One kind of bullant is the 'jumper'. If anything comes near its nest, it jumps out with its jaws snapping. Beware of this ant if you are on a picnic!

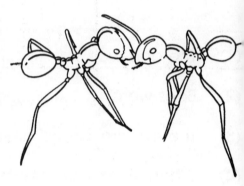

(1)   Bullants are named after an animal called a ....

(2)   Bullants have very powerful jaws or ....

(3)   The stinger is rather like a doctor's ....

(4)   Bullants make nests under logs and ....

(5)   Being larger than other ants, bullants are easily ....

(6)   These ants are hunters and act like .... when attacking.

     Write each word that means:

(7)   strong ....   (8)   more heavy ....

(9)   back ....   (10) put in ....

(11) watch out ....   (12) rushing ....

Set 51   Crossword   (Spelling and Vocabulary)

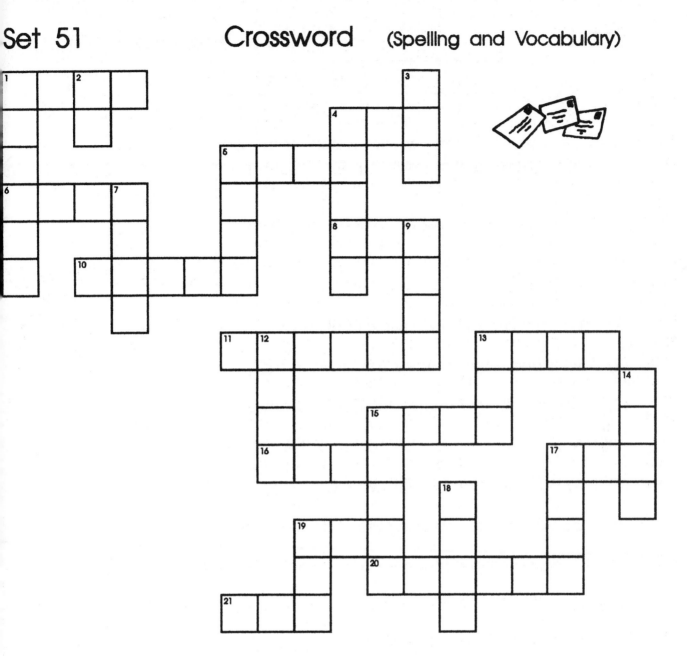

Across

1 We must eat .... to live.
4 slang word for 'policeman'
5 letters and parcels
6 not first
8 juice of plants
10 Noses ..... .
11 They bake bread.
13 not short
15 a small store
16 A ..... is smaller than a city.
17 to move quickly on foot
19 a pixie
20 end
21 It holds water for cattle.

Down

1 Horses live and eat in ..... .
2 not off
3 a large kind of monkey
4 to shut
5 Wheat and corn is ground here.
7 We tell the ..... from clocks.
9 We use ..... to write quick notes.
12 Your father's sister.
13 to cut off
14 A ..... looks after your money.
15 to smell
17 When in a hurry you ..... .
18 A ..... plays music.
19 a kind of tree

Set 52   Shops   (Vocabulary)

delicatessen

cleaner   record   escalator   hardware   hairdresser

counter   mirror   supermarket   newsagent   cafe

hobby

sports   boutique

camera

bakery   butcher

(1)   We buy papers and magazines at a ....

(2)   Men and women have a haircut at the ....

(3)   You can buy women's dresses and other clothes at a ....

(4)   A .... shop sells nails, paints and many kinds of tools.

(5)   To buy a cricket bat you would go into a .... shop.

(6)   Cooked meats and cheeses can be bought at a ....

(7)   To buy a model plane kit you would go to a toy or .... shop.

(8)   A .... shop would sell films and albums.

(9)   The .... sells all kinds of fresh meat.

(10) At the .... you will find fresh bread and cakes.

(11) Mother usually buys all her groceries at the ....

(12) To go upstairs in a large store you use the ....

(13) To pay for goods you go to the shop ....

(14) For a meal or cup of tea you can visit a .... or restaurant.

(15) To see yourself and check if something fits you use a ....

(16) To remove dirt from a suit you go to the dry ....

(17) Taped music is sold at a .... shop.

Ever since people have been on earth they have wanted to fly. Many men tried to copy birds. They began by strapping wings to their backs and trying to take off. Others, as we have read earlier in this book, filled bags with hot air and flew in balloons.

There is an old Greek story about the first man who wanted to fly. His name was Dadalus, who, together with his son Icarus, wanted to fly away from an island. Dadalus made two pairs of wings out of feathers which were stuck together with wax. Off they flew, but unluckily for Icarus, he flew too near the sun. The wax holding the feathers melted and he fell into the ocean.

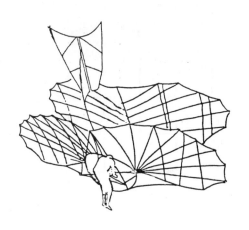

Another man really did make wings from feathers from some chickens. He hoped to fly from Scotland to France. He jumped off a high wall but only fell straight to the ground. 'I should not have used feathers from chickens. Chickens are ground birds and do not fly'.

(1)   People long ago tried to copy .... by flying.

(2)   Dadalus and his son made two .... of wings.

(3)   The wax they used was .... by the sun.

(4)   The two men wanted to fly away from an ....

(5)   The man who wanted to fly from Scotland used feathers from ....

(6)   He took off from a high ....

       Write each word that means:

(7)   wished ....   (8)   tying ....

(9)   before ....   (10) unfortunately ....

(11) actually ....   (12) leapt ....

Set 54　　　Crossword　(Spelling and Vocabulary)

Across
1 I ..... ten dollars for it.
3 Butchers ..... mince meat.
5 begin
7 opposite to 'pull'
8 opposite to 'hot'
10 to run slowly over a distance
11 crazy
12 a lot
14 The sun is ..... on a clear day.
16 space between teeth
18 Children play with them.
21 A ..... has a trunk and branches.
22 We must ..... our best all the time.
24 an animal with flippers

Down
1 a girl's name
2 stop living
4 by yourself
5 We get mutton from ..... .
6 Clothes have a ..... or label.
9 You can beat a ..... .
10 a boy's name
13 every time
14 Some dogs sit and can ..... .
15 You ..... a ball with a bat.
17 You ..... letters.
19 They shine at night.
20 You ..... the table for meals.
23 A road ..... is a plan with
　　names of streets.

Set 55   Space Travel   (Vocabulary)

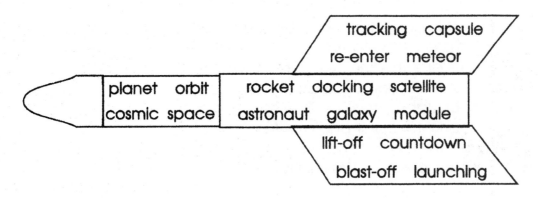

tracking   capsule
re-enter   meteor
planet   orbit
cosmic   space
rocket   docking   satellite
astronaut   galaxy   module
lift-off   countdown
blast-off   launching

(1)   A .... is an object that goes round a planet or star.

(2)   A .... is a huge system of stars and planets in space.

(3)   An .... is a person who travels in space.

(4)   A .... is used to send objects into orbit.

(5)   The time just before a rocket leaves is the ....

(6)   A shooting star is a glowing piece of material called a ....

(7)   The path followed by an object in space is the ....

(8)   Venus is a bright .... of the Sun in the sky.

(9)   .... is the time when a rocket's engines are fired.

(10) Objects in space are watched at a .... station.

(11) People who travel in space ride in a shuttle or ....

(12) When a rocket moves up then .... has taken place.

(13) Travellers in space can contact dangerous .... rays.

(14) When two objects link up in space they are ....

(15) Men explored the Moon in a lunar ....

(16) A rocket leaves the Earth from its .... pad.

(17) To come back to Earth is to .... the atmosphere.

(18) An astronaut wears a .... suit and helmet.

Sharks are not true fish because they have no real bones. Instead of bones they have what scientists call 'cartilage'. They are the vicious hunters of the sea. They devour fish, whales, seals and penguins. Some have been caught, and in their stomachs there have been found tin cans and bottles. In fact they are scavengers that eat almost anything they find. If you give them a chance they may decide to eat you.

A shark never runs out of teeth. As they wear out, or are lost in a fight, more grow up from the gums. A shark's skin is very tough and feels like sandpaper. Not many fish can bite through this covering.

In Sydney, and some other cities, beaches have nets in the sea. They keep the sharks away from swimmers. Rivers and harbours have no nets and the water is often muddy. These are dangerous places to swim. A shark can savage you before you see it.

(1)   Sharks are not true fish because they have no ....

(2)   A large bird that is attacked by sharks is the ....

(3)   Bottles have been found inside the .... of sharks.

(4)   If you touch a shark's skin it feels like ....

(5)   Sydney .... have nets to keep sharks away.

(6)   You should never swim in muddy rivers or ....

Write each word that means:

(7)   real ....

(8)   in place of ....

(9)   eat ....

(10)   opportunity ....

(11)   unsafe ....

(12)   attack and bite ....

Set 57   Crossword   (Spelling and Vocabulary)

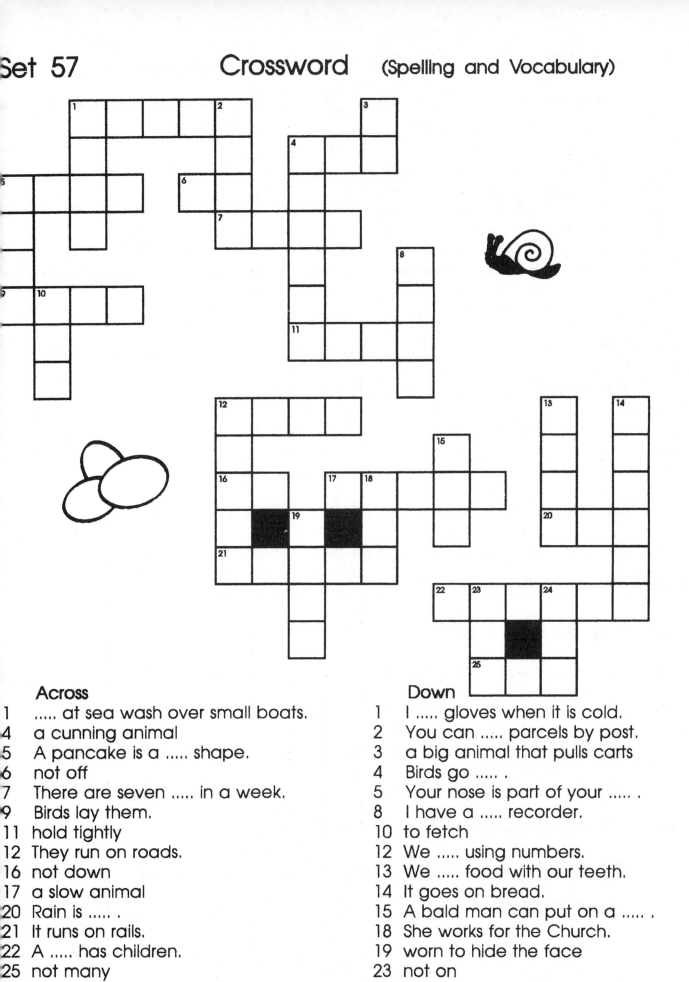

Across

1 ..... at sea wash over small boats.
4 a cunning animal
5 A pancake is a ..... shape.
6 not off
7 There are seven ..... in a week.
9 Birds lay them.
11 hold tightly
12 They run on roads.
16 not down
17 a slow animal
20 Rain is ..... .
21 It runs on rails.
22 A ..... has children.
25 not many

Down

1 I ..... gloves when it is cold.
2 You can ..... parcels by post.
3 a big animal that pulls carts
4 Birds go ..... .
5 Your nose is part of your ..... .
8 I have a ..... recorder.
10 to fetch
12 We ..... using numbers.
13 We ..... food with our teeth.
14 It goes on bread.
15 A bald man can put on a ..... .
18 She works for the Church.
19 worn to hide the face
23 not on
24 ..... old are you?

Set 58   Our Earth   (Vocabulary)

forest	swamp plain rapids
desert spring	volcano lake iceberg
valley equator	cliff stream mountain
meadow coast	island channel

(1)   Land that is often wet and muddy is called a ....

(2)   A .... is a mountain where hot rock and ashes come out.

(3)   A large flat area of land is a ....

(4)   Sheltered land that lies between hills is a ....

(5)   Many trees growing together form a ....

(6)   Places where rivers flow quickly over rocks are called ....

(7)   A large area of inland water is a ....

(8)   Waste dry land in hot areas where little grows is a ....

(9)   A water passage between land is called a ....

(10) An .... is land with water all round it.

(11) The part where land meets the sea is the ....

(12) A .... is a steep rock face that is vertical.

(13) A .... is a young small river that often flows quickly

(14) The hottest part of the earth is at the ....

(15) A .... is a place of clear grassy land for grazing.

(16) A .... is taller than a hill.

(17) An .... is a large chunk of ice floating in the sea.

(18) Water that seeps out from under the ground is a ....

Plants and flowers do not live forever. They make seeds that grow again like themselves. These seeds must not drop close to the parent plant or flower. If they did, then the new plants would find there was not enough room to grow properly. A baby seedling needs to have sunlight for its leaves. Its roots must have plenty of room in the soil to find food and water.

Plants have many different ways of sending their seeds away. Some, like the dandelion and thistle, are taken by the wind. Each little seed has a kind of parachute that helps it float away when the wind is blowing. Others use animals to carry their seeds away. Burrs have hooks on them that stick to the animal's fur. Did you ever find a seed in your sock? Did you pick it off and throw it away? If you did, then you helped the seed to travel and perhaps find its way to some new soil.

Birds like to eat berries and fruits. They too help by dropping the seeds in new places. One palm tree sends its seed by water. The coconut is a palm seed which can float across the ocean from one island to another.

(1)   Plants and .... make seeds which grow.

(2)   Leaves of seedlings need .... to grow.

(3)   Roots of plants find food and .... in the soil.

(4)   The dandelion and the .... are carried by wind.

(5)   Some seeds are carried in the fur of ....

(6)   Birds carry the seeds from berries and ....

(7)   The coconut is a seed that floats on .... waters.

(8)   Burrs are seeds which have .... on them.

       Write each word that means:

(9)   near ....   (10) ride on air or water ....

(11) small ....   (12) ground ....

Set 60   Crossword   (Spelling and Vocabulary)

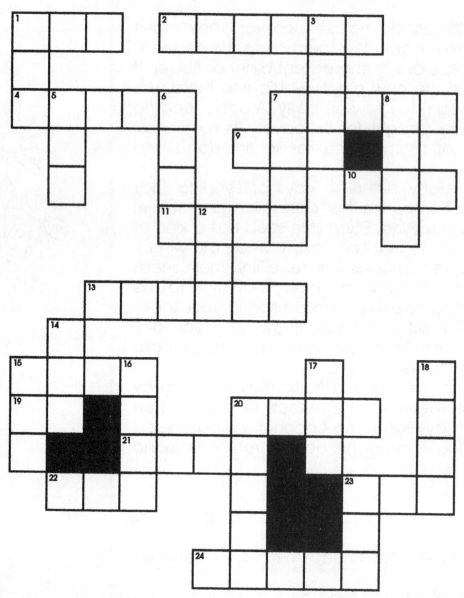

Across
1 We spread it on bread.
2 I ..... a cold in the head.
4 A lion ..... when it is angry.
7 tiny bit of bread
9 aged
10 a single thing
11 Black mixed with white makes ..... .
13 We eat off them.
15 to leap
19 not off
20 Baby rides in it.
21 not any
22 liquid in pens
23 to slope down
24 young boy or girl

Down
1 Food can come in a glass ..... .
3 not soft
5 to have
6 We ..... songs.
7 used to make bricks and cups
8 hair round a lion's neck
12 Sugar makes teeth ..... .
14 We have ..... when we play.
15 A ..... is work to be done.
16 a pretty colour of some shells
17 a small closed truck
18 slightly wet
20 a fruit
23 Father.